HOW TO FAIL AT ALMOST EVERYTHING AND STILL WIN BIG

Kind of the Story of My Life

by Scott Adams

A FastReads Book Summary with
Key Takeaways & Analysis

TABLE OF CONTENTS

BOOK OVERVIEW

In this book, Scott Adams encourages readers to invite failure into their professional lives as it is often the raw material for success. He asserts that no matter how many times you fail, you can come out ahead if you learn something in the process. He maintains that to achieve success, people must optimize their personal energy and position themselves in a way that makes it easy to find luck. He encourages readers to favor systems in place of goals and simplicity in place of optimization.

The book is a humorous narration of the challenges the author encountered while navigating his way through the corporate world. He recounts how he grew from an incompetent worker in a phone company cubicle to the creator of one of the most successful comic strips. Adams draws rich productivity lessons from dozens of personal failures in his businesses and career. Through a depiction of his limited talents, Adams shows that success is not a product of exceptional skill or hard work but a balance of average skills, perseverance and luck.

INTRODUCTION

One of the best ways to increase your odds of success is to manage current opportunities in a way that makes it easy to find luck. The author encourages readers to compare his success story with the accounts of other successful people, note the patterns, and pick up the ideas that work.

Anyone can learn to be successful by filtering strategies that work from the noise of general advice. For starters, you must learn to aggregate the benefits of consistency and simplicity. When seeking the truth, look for consistent patterns in at least two of the six filters for truth: personal experience, common sense, pattern recognition, experiences of other people, expert opinions, and scientific studies. If, for example, experts say that exercise increases productivity and you find (from personal experience) that you get more work done when you work out, you have found a truth.

Creating a clear and simple measure of progress enables you to ascertain whether a strategy is working for you or not. For capitalist ventures, this measure is profit. Profit levels indicate what works and what a business needs to do differently. Finding your human equivalent of profit enables you to simplify complicated decisions. This book provides a model you can use to find your simple measure of success.

CHAPTER ONE: THE TIME I WAS CRAZY

In 2005, Adam's doctor diagnosed him with a mental illness and referred him to a psychologist. In his view, both professionals hinted that he was crazy. He considered the possibility when his blog readers started questioning his mental health. In the months that followed, he lost his ability to speak and, subsequently, became a social outcast. His voice condition jeopardized his career as a professional speaker.

A few months after losing his voice, a client invited him to talk to a mammoth audience in Canada. Despite the potential humiliation he faced, he accepted the invitation to see how his voice would hold up.

CHAPTER TWO: THE DAY OF THE TALK

Although Adams had delivered hundreds of talks before, this event was unique in that, for the first time in his career, he wondered if he could speak. He knew that his reputation as a professional speaker was at stake if the audience did not understand anything he said. Adam asserts that he had put himself in this position because he had learned to appreciate, invite and survive failure. He encouraged failure because he knew he could profit from it. He intended to use this event to understand why his voice worked in some situations and failed in others.

Although his voice was not very good, he managed to hold the attention of the audience and deliver his speech. He lost his ability to speak again when he walked off the stage. From this experience, he discovered that the problem was not with his vocal cords but with his mind. Adams concedes that he learned everything he knows about overcoming failure in the three years it took him to find a solution to his voice problem.

CHAPTER THREE: PASSION IS BULLSHIT

"Follow your passion" is not only one of the most popular pieces of advice, but also one of the most misleading. Passion may motivate you, give you perseverance, and even make you persuasive. But if you pursue a goal purely out of passion, you are in it for the wrong reason. Passion pushes people to take big risks in the pursuit of unreasonable goals. The result is often a huge success or a massive failure. People who accomplish massive feats talk about passion as the key to their success because it is suitably humble and accessible to everyone. Those who fail never talk about it.

Passion is a misleading motivator because it is usually the result, rather the cause, of success. The average person becomes passionate about mundane projects when the likelihood of success increases. When things start falling apart, passion often gives way to frustration.

You can think of passion as a natural by-product of talent as people tend to be passionate about things they are good at. It is easy to assume that someone is good at something because he or she is passionate about it. In truth, most people are passionate about what they do because they are good at what they do. Often, personal energy is a better predictor of success than passion.

CHAPTER FOUR: SOME OF MY MANY FAILURES IN SUMMARY FORM

Successful people consciously look for failure because they know this is where success hides. When you view failure as a tool – rather than an outcome – every challenge makes you smarter, stronger and more energized. From this perspective, success is still attainable even if you fail in 95 percent of the things you try.

Over the course of three decades, the author ventured into and failed in a long series of jobs and businesses. Adams narrates how he published a meditation guide, designed two computer games, developed a psychic practice program, created a modem-to-modem file transfer program, and opened a chain of restaurants. Most of these ventures failed because their execution flopped or the original idea turned out to be sophomoric. He admits that these failures taught him some valuable lessons:

• Good ideas are not marketable because the world is full of them. Concentrate on developing ideas you can execute well.

• Look for opportunities where you have a natural advantage. Leverage your talents.

• Learn as much as you can about the business you are in.

• Transfer the knowledge gained from your failures to ventures with higher probabilities of success.

• Try different things until you get the timing right. Success is often the result of good timing, which is difficult to predict with a narrow line of products.

• Every idea you execute, regardless of how it ends, generates numerous benefits in knowledge and talent.

• A shareholder cannot trust a company's management to deliver useful information. Diversify your portfolio to hedge your bets.

• Partner with people or businesses that are in your prospective line of business.

CHAPTER FIVE: MY ABSOLUTE FAVORITE SPECTACULAR FAILURE

Most failures involve bad judgment, ignorance or bad luck. Adams admits that his favorite failure combined all three mishaps. In his senior year in college, he landed an interview with one of the biggest accounting firms in New York. Despite the freezing winter weather, he decided not to carry a jacket as he wouldn't be staying for long. His second mistake was going for the interview in his casual college attire. The interviewer turned him away the moment he walked in.

On his way home, he took a new route through a valley in the Catskill Mountains. Miles into the highway, the car's engine died, and he steered the car to the roadside. With no cars on the road, no sign of life for miles, and no jacket in sub-zero temperatures, he knew he had hit rock bottom.

As the temperature dropped in his car, he figured that his only option was to run in the direction he was headed. Just when he felt he couldn't go any further, a shoe salesman in a station wagon appeared in the blizzard and saved his life. A few months later, he traded the car for a one-way ticket to Northern California. Adams reckons that this was one of the best decisions he ever made.

CHAPTER SIX: GOALS VERSUS SYSTEMS

On his flight to California, Adams met an elderly businessman who volunteered some career advice. He confided in Adams that whenever he landed a new job, he immediately went in search for a better one because job seeking was – for him – an ongoing process. He let Adams know that his job was not his job; his job was to always be on the lookout for a better deal.

Over the years, having a system for looking for better deals worked remarkably well for the businessman. As he hopped from job to job, he gained tremendous experience and, ultimately, became the CEO of a screw-making company. If he had started out with specific goals in mind, his career path would have been very limited. His system was simple: the new job had to be better than the last job and offer new knowledge that would enable him to make the next hop.

Systems-driven people outperform goal-oriented people because they never lose a sense of purpose or direction. Setting goals sets you on a losing path because until you achieve your goal, you will be living in a state of near-continuous failure. When you achieve the goal, you lose the one thing that motivated you to work. If things never work out, a goal-oriented person faces permanent failure. A system-driven person maintains his energy because he succeeds every time he applies his system.

Unlike a goal, which has a specific end, a system is a set of activities you do on a regular basis to increases your chances of success. In a typical system model, you develop a system of eating right, rather than a goal of losing a specific number of pounds. You decide to be a serial entrepreneur, rather than focus on the goal of making a million dollars.

Key Takeaways

• Your job is not your job. Always be on the lookout for better options.

• Most successful people follow systems, not goals. Systems have no deadlines or predictable results but, implemented well, they almost guarantee success.

• Identify your core skills and develop a system that builds on these skills to increase your chances of success in your field.

CHAPTER SEVEN: MY SYSTEM

While in college, Adams decided to develop a system that would utilize his talents. He figured that all he wanted to do was create and run a business. His entrepreneurial plan included completing an economics degree, securing a job at a major bank, and learning all he could about business from his job. The skills he acquired would enable him to create a product that was easy to produce in unlimited quantities.

He identified creativity as his competitive edge and resolved to pursue several artistic ventures until the public appreciated his genius. He knew the system would subject him to numerous failures in the short term. Still, he reckoned that the system would make it easy to find luck in the long term. He concedes that had he pursued specific goals instead, he would have given up too early. With a system, he could grow his capabilities and march on regardless of the fate of the last project.

Key Takeaways

• Make practical plans and stick to them.

• At the very least, develop a general strategy for your life and focus on working on it every day.

CHAPTER EIGHT: MY CORPORATE CAREER FIZZLED

After landing in California, Adams walked into a branch of Crocker National Bank, asked for a job, and immediately got hired as a teller. As it were, his degree in economics made him overqualified for the job. However, his ineptitude at keeping track of transactions almost cost him the job. Within the eight years that he worked at the bank, he moved from being a teller to a branch management trainee, lending officer, project manager, budget supervisor, among other roles. He admits that he failed in one job after another. Interestingly, his career at the bank ended not because of his incompetence, but because the bank could no longer promote white males in line with its diversity program.

While working for Crocker, Adams interviewed for a budgeting role at a local phone company and got the job. He managed to finish the evening MBA classes he had been taking at Berkeley while holding the new job. With his new qualification, he figured that he was a serious contender for a district manager position that had opened up. As luck would have it, a senior executive disclosed to him that the company had implemented a diversity program and would not be promoting white males in the foreseeable future. With the prospects of an upper management role gone, Adams decided to revive his cartooning interest.

CHAPTER NINE: DECIDING VERSUS WANTING

A lot of people wish for success, riches and fame. A few of these people find out what their ambition will cost, make a commitment to pay the price, and take action. For the rest, wishful thinking ends where it started: in the mind. When you decide to be successful, you acknowledge the sacrifices needed to make your dream a reality and you start paying the price. The sacrifices may include pursuing laborious courses, spending less time with your children, or taking enormous business risks. In most cases, this price is negotiable. If you pick a favorable system, the price comes down to within your budget.

CHAPTER TEN: THE SELFISHNESS ILLUSION

In your bid to balance your needs with those of others, you will fall into one of the three groups of people in the world: the selfish, the stupid, and those who are a burden on others. Being selfish is your best bet. This means spending most of your time on yourself – on your health, career and personal relationships. Generosity is a problematic concept because it causes people to think only on the short term. Taking care of yourself will make you better suited to help others over the long term. Selfishness is a necessary precursor to success.

Key Takeaways

• Generous people take care of themselves first.

• Pursue your objectives selfishly and your focus will turn outward in time.

• When you meet all your personal needs, the inclination to helps others will be instinctive.

CHAPTER ELEVEN: THE ENERGY METRIC

To manage multiple priorities, make choices that maximize your personal energy. This means having something to look forward to each day, keeping fit, eating healthy, getting enough sleep, and avoiding unnecessary stress. Commanding good energy not only improves your career, but also your social and family lives. At its most basic, energy is anything that gives you a positive physical or mental lift.

Adams admits that despite working in awful corporate jobs, he enjoyed going to work because he exercised most evenings and had side projects that promised a better future. He divulges that writing, especially to help others, motivates him and keeps his energy levels up.

To optimize your personal energy, you must maximize it in all areas of your life and focus on the big picture. Some activities, such as having an extra cocktail, may boost your energy for the night, but they are not sustainable over the long term.

Individually, the actions you take to increase your personal energy may seem selfish. However, these actions add up to something with profound benefits in the long run. People may not appreciate your lateness when you take time to do something that energizes you, but they will appreciate the energy you bring with you.

Matching Mental State to Activity

To maximize your productivity, try matching your mental state to the task at hand. If you are creative in the morning, tackle tasks that require creativity. If you find that you struggle with mental blocks in late afternoons but still have some physical energy left, try exercising. If, like most people, you don't have a flexible schedule, try waking up early in the morning. Productivity levels usually peak during this period. It may take some time to get used to waking up at 4.00 A.M. but once you do, it will be effortless.

Simplifiers Versus Optimizers

Simplifiers look for the easiest way to tackle a task, knowing well that more effort may produce better outcomes. Optimizers look for the best solution to a problem, even if the complexity of the solution introduces more opportunities for things to go wrong. For simplifiers, optimizing can be exhausting because it requires full concentration.

Knowing which situation calls for simplification and which requires optimization can be challenging. As a rule, any situation that involves communication with others requires simplification. If it's a project you can do by yourself or with a partner you get along with, optimization may be a better option. If you can't decide what plan will work better, go with the simple one. If you estimate that the cost of failure of a project will be high, develop a simple plan to minimize opportunities for failure.

When choosing a system to use, pick a simple one. You can optimize and perfect it as it becomes effortless and successful. Very few people have the willpower to implement complex plans. Maintaining the high levels of energy needed to implement a complex plan may also prove difficult in the long run. Simplification also frees up time and energy and makes tasks easier to complete. However, it's important to note that you cannot simplify every task. It helps to view simplification as a long-term goal.

On Body Posture, Tidiness, and Knowledge

Your brain picks cues from your body language to decide whether to lazy off or concentrate on a task. Assign specific spaces and sitting positions to work and leisure and draw clear demarcations. You can change how you feel and think simply by changing your position and environment.

Although tidiness is mostly a personal choice, clearing items and miscellaneous tasks on your workstation can make you more energetic and clearheaded. Consider inviting people to your working area on a regular basis. Their presence may inspire you to unclutter your space.

The fear that you don't have sufficient knowledge to execute a career plan or business idea is one of the biggest obstacles to success. Before you assume that something will be too hard to learn in reasonable time, ask questions. Often, you'll discover that there's an easy solution waiting. Do some flash research and you will find that millions of people have wondered about the same thing, and a few have simplified and packaged the solution.

Priorities

Your priorities are concentric circles, much like the ones archers use to practice. As these priorities are bound to overlap, it is your duty to develop a simple rule to manage conflicting interests. Often, you will know you made the right choice if it increases your personal energy.

• The bull's eye, which is your biggest priority, is you. Take care of your health first.

• The second-biggest priority is your personal finance – your investments, job and assets.

• The third ring is your family, friends, and other personal relationships.

• The subsequent rings are your local community, nation, and the rest of the world.

Key Takeaways

• A simple system is your best bet for achieving success. You can optimize it to increase value after you become successful.

• To increase productivity, focus on maximizing your personal energy, not the tasks you have to perform.

• To maximize your energy, focus on yourself first: your fitness, health and sleep. Then take care of your personal finances and relationships – in that order.

CHAPTER TWELVE: MANAGING YOUR ATTITUDE

Your attitude is a product of your health, thoughts and environment. By manipulating these constraints, you can improve your attitude, increase your productivity, and enjoy life more. To elevate your attitude:

• Focus on food, exercise and sleep. Before anything else, get these right.

• Increase your happy thoughts and try to eliminate disturbing thoughts. Practice daydreaming and avoid depressing media, especially the news.

• Work on projects that can help others, change the world, or make you really rich.

• Smile, even if you have to fake it. Forcing a smile can trigger happiness, just as acting confident can make you feel confident.

• Practice until you become good at unimportant things such as sports or hobbies. You'll develop a success habit that spills over to important things.

• Adopt a practical illusion. If putting on certain clothes or partaking in a certain ritual makes you energized, roll with it.

Key Takeaways

• When you can't change reality, you can always change your point of view. Don't hesitate to change you perception to something that makes you happy.

• To develop a positive attitude, pay attention to your health, avoid downing people and events, and adopt a motivating delusion.

CHAPTER THIRTEEN: IT'S ALREADY WORKING

The first filter for success is a desire to seek knowledge. You're on your way to success if you can identify with people who think about and study the mechanics of success. You become who you act.

CHAPTER FOURTEEN: MY PINKIE GOES NUTS

When the comic strip, Dilbert, was still in its infancy, Adams developed focal dystonia – a condition that made his pinkie finger spasm whenever he tried to draw. An expert on the condition advised him to quit his drawing job as there was no known cure. During a follow-up visit, the doctor asked if Adams would like to be part of an experimental treatment and he agreed. The therapies did not work, and Adams was forced to learn to draw with his left hand. Over the course of several weeks, he practiced drawing motions that involved pulling away his hand from paper before the spasm started. Using this exercise, he rewired his brain, overcame a condition that had no cure, and went back to drawing with his right hand.

CHAPTER FIFTEEN: MY SPEAKING CAREER

At one point, a representative for a petroleum organization in Canada called Adams and asked him to go and deliver a speech. Due to his tight schedule and the logistics involved, he declined the offer. The representative pressured him to name any price he wanted. If he asked for a very large sum, she would go back to the organization and say she tried. Adams did some research and figured that if he asked for $5,000, the organization would withdraw the offer. Amusingly, the organization settled for the price and offered to pay for first-class travel and hotel expenses.

Over time, Adams progressively raised his fees to $10,000, $25,000 and, eventually, $45,000. At some point, he declined an offer for $100,000 for a one hour speech on a topic of his choosing. He credits his success to a friend who advised him to overprice his services and see what happened.

Key Takeaways

• To a significant extent, your success depends on who you know. The people in your professional circles do not need to be influential CEOs. A friend with a different perspective will do.

CHAPTER SIXTEEN: MY VOICE PROBLEM GETS A NAME

When Adams lost his voice in 2005, he consulted numerous specialists – all of whom were unfamiliar with his condition. He decided to consult the internet, but all the search terms he used were too broad to give a definite diagnosis. Eventually, he discovered it was a classic case of spasmodic dystonia – a condition characterized by clipped syllables and broken words. An expert in the condition told him that there was no cure, but he was determined to become the first person to find a solution.

CHAPTER SEVENTEEN: THE VOICE SOLUTION THAT DIDN'T WORK

In a bid to restore his voice, Adams tried the standard treatment for spasmodic dystonia. The treatment included a shot of Botox through the front of his neck every few weeks. The first treatment worked well for him, but subsequent shots were less effective. He decided to stop the treatment and pursue a permanent fix on his own.

CHAPTER EIGHTEEN: RECOGNIZING YOUR TALENTS AND KNOWING WHEN TO QUIT

How do you identify your talent or the skills you can combine to succeed at something?

• Try to recall the activities you obsessively participated in before you were ten years old. Childhood compulsions do not guarantee talent, but they point to preferences that become skills.

• Find activities for which you had a high tolerance for risk when growing up. Your risk profile is often a predictor of talent.

• Try doing a lot of things. If these things are entrepreneurial ventures, abandon them when they take too long to pan out. Persistent is an important skill, but know when to quit. If it starts well, it will go well. The opposite is true.

The enthusiasm model is an effective tool for predicting the success of a product or service. If a subset of the public enthusiastically picks up on your idea right away, you are set for success. Over time, a product that elicits the excitement of the public evolves to become a quality product. Quality is a luxury that often comes after public acceptance, which usually funds future improvements.

Key Takeaways

• You can identify your talents from your childhood obsessions and the activities for which you took significant risks.

• Failure is often a product of bad luck, but bad luck is seldom consistent. When you try again, the odds are in your favor.

• Move on to something different if your idea, art or product does not excite anyone (other than your family and friends) in the beginning.

CHAPTER NINETEEN: IS PRACTICE YOUR THING?

While practice is a vital component of success, deciding what to practice is far more important. It makes little sense to practice something that has no economic value or that does not add to your bottom line. Practicing often comes naturally to some people, but others consider it a torturous form of repetition. Whichever side you fall into, you can ease the process by creating a practice plan that embraces your natural inclinations.

If you are not a practicer, you can pursue a novelty venture in lieu of a goal that requires constant repetition. For example, you may consider becoming a designer, entrepreneur, or even a doctor. In each of these professions, your skills increase with experience rather than practice.

CHAPTER TWENTY: MANAGING YOUR ODDS FOR SUCCESS

To become successful, you must pick a good system and pursue it until luck finds you. Every skill you acquire along the way doubles your chances of becoming successful. The best part is that you don't have to master the skills you acquire; you merely need to be good at more than one skill. In its simplest form, the success formula would be:

Good + good = Excellent

Assuming that you are not a world-class performer in one skill, your chances of success are better if you are good in two skills than excellent at one. Although some skills will be more valuable than others, you will motivate yourself if you think of each skill you acquire as an addition to your odds of success. The belief that each skill will double your odds of success may not be accurate, but it increases the odds that you will act.

The more you know, the more you can know

You can also increase your odds of success by learning as much as possible in different fields. Even if you won't put to practical use what you learn, your knowledge will make it easier to understand other things. To ease the process, start by exposing yourself to topics you find interesting.

Key Takeaways

• Each skill you acquire doubles your odds of becoming successful.

• When it comes to skills, choose quantity over quality.

• If you think a skill might add some value to your portfolio, try, at the very least, to learn the basics.

CHAPTER TWENTY ONE: THE MATH OF SUCCESS

Although you can't directly control your luck, you can increase your odds of success. As with any other success strategy, finding your odds in life is difficult because you have some blind spots. It helps to view the world from a mathematical perspective and work towards finding these blind spots. If you find yourself going from failure to failure in business or in your personal life, you can find a pattern if you look at the right places.

To increase your odds of success, work on becoming good at skills that go well together and which are useful for your work. You give luck a good chance of finding you if you possess a working knowledge of the following skills: public speaking, business writing, proper grammar, second language, accounting, design and persuasion. Being merely good in psychology, accounting, conversation, overcoming shyness, and technology also increases your chances of success. As most people do not always have an accurate view of their potential, you may find that you feel different when you train in one of these skills, particularly public speaking. Often, the only way you can know how much potential you have is to test yourself.

Psychology will help you understand that:

• The quality of something is dependent on your point of reference.

• Cause and effect drive people's decisions. Reason is often the smallest driver of behavior. People are mostly irrational and make most of their decisions based on how they feel about something.

Some specialties, such as design, are rule-based. You need not have any talent to grasp the essentials. Conversation skills are also learnable and can help you become better at persuading and influencing other people. Learning accounting will give you the good judgment of executing ideas that work on paper.

You can also learn to overcome shyness just like you learn to swim. Some important tips to remember are:

• Act like a confident person you know. Faking confidence will make you confident.

• Most people feel awkward in social situations at some point. Remember that on the inside, no one has it all together – some people have just learned to hide it well.

• Practice. Put yourself in situations that may embarrass you and exercise your ego.

No matter how educated you are, you risk coming out as incompetent if your grammar is lacking. Considering how easy it is to fix grammar flaws, it is well worth the effort. Decisiveness is also an important skill because people often see it as a mark of leadership – no matter how many doubts you have on the inside.

Persuasion skills play a big part in getting ahead – no matter the profession you choose. To learn persuasion skills, find books on the topic and practice persuading people in your personal and business interactions. Some powerful persuasion phrases include: "because," "I'm not interested," "I don't do that," and "would you mind?" Ensure that you only persuade people to do what is in their interest.

Acquiring proper voice techniques means using the right tone, breath control and mouth strategies. Voice quality not only makes you attractive to potential partners, but also increases your chances of climbing the corporate ladder. People with stronger voices tend to appear more capable than they are and, subsequently, secure greater management abilities. To develop your best success voice:

• Practice breathing from the bottom of your lungs – you will sound more confident.

• Pick a tone. The best tone is usually higher than your default tone. High-pitched voices penetrate background noises but low tones carry hints of seriousness.

• Hum the first part of the "Happy Birthday" song and use your natural voice thereafter. Although the effect will only last a while, your voice will sounder smoother than normal.

• Stand or sit straight to get your best voice out.

• Fake confidence by imagining you are a confident person and speaking as he or she would.

• Practice until you get rid of hawing, hemming, and anything else that disrupts the flow of your speech. Try developing sentences in your mind before speaking.

Key Takeaways

• Skill mastery is not essential for success – you simply need to be good at something.

• Make a list of skills you consider essential for success in your profession, take time to learn the basics, and combine the skills to increase your odds of success.

• Get essential skills like psychology right and things will start working out. In a series of failures, there is always a pattern you can identify and correct if you possess the right set of skills.

CHAPTER TWENTY-TWO: PATTERN RECOGNITION

A vital component of success is the ability to identify patterns in all areas of life. Identifying patterns changes your thoughts on your chances of succeeding and, subsequently, improves your performance. To become successful, start by adopting the patterns of highly effective people that Stephen Covey identifies:

1. Be proactive.

2. Think about good outcomes when you begin working on a project.

3. Prioritize.

4. Adopt a win-win approach.

5. Try to understand others before trying to make them understand you.

6. Harness the power of teamwork.

7. Don't stop learning.

Other components of success include exercise, courage, and education. Exercise builds up the energy, creativity and motivation you need to succeed. Courage enables you to take leaps of faith and venture into areas that others deem too risky. Learn to face and handle failure, rejection and embarrassment. When you get the right kind of education, your chances of success increase dramatically.

Key Takeaways

• To become successful, identify the patterns of successful people and apply them to your life.

• Success is a learnable skill; get the right education, exercise at least five days a week, and get your psychological bravery up.

CHAPTER TWENTY-THREE: HUMOR

Having a sense of humor not only makes you seem attractive, but also raises your energy levels. A sense of humor also makes your daily troubles bearable and increases your creativity. Effort matters a lot for anyone trying to dispense a bit of humor. Although the quality of the story is not very important, anyone trying to pass along some humor should avoid puns and wordplay, complaining too much, mocking people, and overly deprecating the self.

If you are going to tell a joke, know your audience first. Some people prefer to laugh about bad things happening to others and some prefer stories with clever twists. Observe what your audience talks and laughs about to gauge the general inclination.

CHAPTER TWENTY-FOUR: AFFIRMATIONS

Affirmations are statements you repeat to yourself when you want to achieve something. You can write, speak or think about the outcomes you would like to accomplish. The content of the affirmations does not matter much – the chief objective is to increase your focus on your goals. While the workings of affirmations are not well known, these statements have the potential to propel you to accomplish your grandest dreams. Adams admits that one of his affirmations: "I, Scott Adams, will be a famous cartoonist" enabled him to achieve his most desirable job.

CHAPTER TWENTY-FIVE: TIMING IS LUCK TOO

When affirmations work for you, you will feel like you stumbled on a rare case of luck. While there are numerous components of luck, the biggest, by far, is timing. When your timing is off, all of your talents and efforts may be futile. You can prepare yourself by making learning a continuous commitment, pursuing several ventures, and keeping an optimistic eye.

Key Takeaways

• Channel your time, energy and focus into meaningful ventures and keep trying until you hit a lucky spot.

• If you stay in the game long enough, the world will guarantee your success.

CHAPTER TWENTY-SIX: A FEW TIMES AFFIRMATIONS WORKED

Adams divulges that prior to the publication of his book, The Dilbert Principle, he visualized himself as a best-selling author. The book, together with a follow-up volume, went on to become number one and two respectively on the New York Times non-fiction bestseller list. He speculates that the failure of the animated Dilbert TV show had something to do with his reluctance to use affirmations when he worked as the co-executive producer of the show. Still, he asserts that his affirmations only worked when he had an unabated desire for success.

Key Takeaways

• Affirmations only work when you are 100 percent committed to the success of a venture.

CHAPTER TWENTY-SEVEN: VOICE UPDATE

Months after quitting Botox shots, Adams' voice became so weak that he couldn't pursue his speaking career, talk to people in social events, or even order food at a restaurant. He tried alternative therapies such as acupuncture, mineral supplements, and stutter cures – all with no success. He tried to identify the relationship between his voice patterns and his diet, sleep and exercise, but no patterns emerged. He also researched the condition and set his phone to receive email notifications whenever someone mentioned the condition on the Internet. Most of the updates only mentioned the incurability of the condition. All the same, he kept his optimism and the affirmation that he would speak perfectly again.

CHAPTER TWENTY-EIGHT: EXPERTS

Experts can get it wrong the first time. In his late twenties, for example, Adams was misdiagnosed with a form of neck cancer. From his observations, experts are mostly right on easy matters. When the subject matter is new, complex or mysterious, experts are only right half of the time. Pattern recognition and a healthy dose of optimism can give you an idea of when an expert is wrong. If your intuition tells you that a professional is wrong, don't ignore it.

CHAPTER TWENTY-NINE: ASSOCIATION PROGRAMMING

Humans are social beings who absorb the energy and character traits of those around them. If you look closely, you will notice patterns everywhere:

• Studies indicate that hanging around overweight people can cause you to gain weight.

• Recovering alcoholics who don't cut ties with their drinking buddies tend to relapse.

• Alongside Adams, two other employees who worked at Pacific Bell ended up becoming published writers.

The people you associate with make a huge difference in your life. They may give you some vital information, encourage you to pursue a venture, or nudge you in the right direction with some positive criticism. If you associate with successful people, their habits (and, in extension, their success), is bound to rub off on you. Essentially, you can reprogram your brain by spending time with the people who represent the person you would like to become.

Key Takeaways

• Associate with the people you want to become because success, optimism and toxic habits tend to rub off on you.

• To change yourself, spend time around people with the character you seek.

CHAPTER THIRTY: HAPPINESS

Your ultimate goal in life is the maximization of your happiness. At its most basic, happiness is a feeling of pleasant sensations. Contrary to popular belief, your situation and circumstances only account for about 20 percent of your happiness. About 80 percent of your happiness comes from your body chemistry – which you can manipulate. You can influence your body chemistry with medical pills and other drugs, but this method comes with adverse risks. The natural approach involves altering your lifestyle to invite positive thoughts. To manipulate your body chemistry and find happiness, consider doing the following:

• Partake in activities you want to, when you want to. It's easier to find happiness in timing than in the resources you have. Adopt a flexible schedule that allows you to indulge in your favorite activities. Consider flexibility a vital factor when making any major life decision.

• Consider where you are going and do things that increase your skills. Happiness has a lot to do with where you are headed. Before settling for a career, consider whether it will lead to an increase in your skills.

• Cultivate positive imagination. Imagining a bright future boosts your personal energy and increases your happiness. Paint a mental picture of a spectacular future – a picture that is not hinged on your reality.

• Eat well, sleep well, and exercise.

When mastered, these elements attract other components of happiness such as career success, a soulmate, and a feeling of importance.

Key Takeaways

• Happiness is 20 percent what happens to you and 80 percent what you make happen.

• Happiness comes naturally when you adopt a flexible schedule and a healthy lifestyle, imagine a positive future, and increase your competence.

• To maximize your happiness, watch your diet, exercise and sleep. Adopt a routine and help others.

CHAPTER THIRTY-ONE: DIET

While Adams cautions his readers against following his dietary advice, he contends that the secret to healthy dieting is simple: eat as much of anything as you want, when you want. The trick is in choosing to want to eat the right foods. Your hunger level, age, and the technique you use to prepare food affect your taste preferences. You can reprogram these preferences and start eating whatever you want. To kick start the process:

Look at things differently. Think of your body as a programmable unit that takes in food and gives out feelings and thoughts. What you eat affects your personal energy levels, mood, and problem-solving ability. Note what you eat and how you feel afterwards. Take the experiment a notch higher by skipping some foods and taking note of your mood. Identify the foods that make you energetic and those that make you sleepy.

View food as a component that fuels exercise. The traditional view that one needs to eat well and exercise to stay fit is misleading because food and exercise are not equal partners. When you eat carbs, you are more likely to sleep than exercise. You must eat right first to be in the mood for exercise. People fail when they try to change their diets and exercise at the same time because both activities require immense willpower.

Eat as much of anything that is not carbs. This way, you save the willpower you use to avoid overeating and use it to avoid the wrong kinds of food. When you allow yourself to eat as much as possible of any food that is not junk, resisting the junk food no longer seems very difficult. Do this for each type of bad food for a few months. You may gain weight in the short term, but you will lose your addiction in the long run.

Make eating healthy food convenient by stocking up on fruits, vegetables, fish and other healthy foods. Allow yourself to eat as much of these foods as you can to save your willpower.

Know why you eat. If your hunger sensations don't go away, it could be because you are tired or sleepy. Work on fixing non-hunger issues before you overeat. If you have to partake in social eating, go for foods with low calories.

Make healthy foods tasty by adding flavor with condiments and seasonings such as soy sauce, pepper, garlic, curry and vegetable broth. Experiment with a wide range of seasonings until you find what works for you.

Adopt a lifestyle that encourages healthy eating. Consider spending more time with fit people.

Consider drinking two to four cups of coffee a day. Coffee increases your energy levels and makes you more alert and productive.

Find happiness in other areas of your life and it will be easier to stick to a good diet. Success and happiness have a way of spilling over to other areas of your life.

Key Takeaways

• To reprogram your taste preferences, look for the relationship between what you eat and how you feel, and learn to associate bad foods with bad moods.

• Avoiding bad foods and exercising at the same time require unsustainable amounts of willpower. Get your diet right first and you will have the energy to exercise.

• Save the willpower you need to avoid bad foods by allowing yourself to eat as much of the good foods as you can.

• Remove bad food from your home and stock up on good food.

• Develop a system, not goals, to reach your ideal weight.

CHAPTER THIRTY-TWO: FITNESS

Exercise is hard work – especially when you try to fit it into a routine already filled with work and family. Still, it is possible to develop a system that works. Some pointers include:

• Be active every day, in some way. Take a walk, play a sport, or even clean. It doesn't matter how much exercise you get. What matters is that you are forming a habit.

• Simplify your exercise routines to a level that does not feel like work. Take leisure walks or some other form of exercise you enjoy until it becomes habitual. Don't interrupt the habit with breaks between days.

• Avoid setting distance or time-based exercise goals – you will be setting yourself up for failure. The key is to develop a system, not goals.

• If you are married, you can schedule your exercise by exercising together, exercising at the same time each day, and joining an organized team with a fixed schedule.

• Exercise to a level that is just enough for the day. Light exercises motivate you and increase your energy levels.

• After exercise, reward yourself with healthy foods or routines you enjoy.

• If you don't feel like exercising, reprogram your mind by manipulating your cues. Putting on exercise clothes, for example, can boost your energy and make exercising desirable. You can also trick yourself into working out by giving yourself permission to walk into a gym, look around, and leave.

Key Takeaways

• Keep fit every day by adopting an exercise routine that is simple and easy to follow through.

• Tailor your fitness plan to your preferences. An expert's plan will not work for you.

CHAPTER THIRTY-THREE: VOICE UPDATE 2

Three years after losing his voice, Adams was barely positive about the possibility of finding a cure. Nevertheless, he continued affirming that he would speak perfectly again. One day, he found out that a doctor in Japan had been successful in treating the condition with a surgical procedure. After consulting with experts in spasmodic dysphonia, he discovered that another doctor was pioneering another form of neck surgery in Los Angeles. Adams, who was skeptical about the effectiveness of this procedure, arranged meetings with some of the doctor's past patients. When he discovered that they could talk perfectly, he scheduled the procedure.

CHAPTER THIRTY-FOUR: LUCK

If you track all success to its inception, you will find that it is nothing more than pure luck. If some of the most successful people in the world (such as Bill Gates and Warrant Buffet) had been born in a different time, their skills, personality and perseverance would not have matched the opportunities around them. You increase your odds of success by adding up on your knowledge, skills and perseverance.

CHAPTER THIRTY-FIVE: CALENDAR TREE START-UP

While he was still creating Dilbert comics, Adams worked on a website that allowed users to create events and share them with their teammates. The startup was getting ready for launch at the time of writing this book. Adams confesses that juggling his cartoonist career with his blog, book and startup required a lot of mental energy. The key to muster this energy is to eat well, exercise, and adopt a flexible schedule.

Adams' system involves two aspects: first, getting his mental and physical energy right and, second, pursuing multiple ventures to increase the odds of finding luck. Calendar Tree is a product of this approach. Adams reckons that regardless of whether the startup succeeds or fails, he will gain several capable contacts and a substantial knowledge of the startup process and other procedures.

CHAPTER THIRTY-SIX: VOICE UPDATE 3

After the surgery, Adams struggled with a strange disconnect between his brain and vocal cords. Three and a half months into his recovery, he started talking – albeit in a weak and breathy voice. His voice improved steadily in subsequent months. Years later, he ended up with a voice that was better than ever before. He encourages people struggling with seemingly incurable conditions to re-estimate their odds of recovery. A change in attitude can make all the difference.

CHAPTER THIRTY SEVEN: A FINAL NOTE ABOUT AFFIRMATIONS

Affirmations are not an exact science; they are a mystery, much like positive thinking, visualizations and prayers. However, affirmations tend to work better than positive thinking – for logical reasons that the human brain may not understand. You do not need to have detailed affirmations or practice on a regular or prolonged basis; you merely need to have a consistent focus on what you want to achieve. The goal of affirmations is to increase your focus, boost your energy, and motivate you to work on your system. Keep affirmations broad enough to increase your chances of finding luck.

CHAPTER THIRTY-EIGHT: SUMMARY

In summary:

• The first step towards success is to eat good foods so that you can get the energy to exercise. Exercise increases your personal energy and, subsequently, makes you more productive, creative and capable of problem-solving.

• The second step is finding luck. While you can't control your luck, you can learn to identify patterns and move from strategies with bad odds to those with good odds. Work on increasing your skills, avoid career traps, and in whichever venture you pursue, persevere long enough for luck to find you.

• Happiness, which is the ultimate goal, will come naturally when you work on getting good health, a flexible schedule, and resources.

• Some skills increase your odds of success more than others. Work on acquiring key skills such as public speaking, simplification, basic accounting, business writing, the psychology of persuasion, and good grammar.

• Think of yourself as a programmable robot; when you think, eat, and exercise well, you invite good outcomes.

• Try to find patterns of success or failure in your life. Do some research and experiment on yourself until you find what works for you.

• Remember that successful people work with systems, not goals, and that failure is your friend.

Summary of Ego is the Enemy: by Ryan Holiday

Summary of Tribe: by Sebastian Junger

Summary of You Are a Badass: by Jen Sincero

Summary of Grit: by Angela Duckworth

Made in the USA
Lexington, KY
31 May 2017